Legal Business
Starting your Own Profitable Law Office

Table of Contents

Chapter 1. Introduction

Unleashing your entrepreneurial spirit in the world of legal practice is no small feat! Our Special Report on "Legal Business: Starting your Own Profitable Law Office" is just what you need to navigate this complex endeavor. This comprehensive guide is filled with insider knowledge, practical advice and tested strategies that can aid you in establishing a successful, financially thriving law practice. It allows you to understand the intricacies of the legal business, strategize to overcome challenges, get a grip on financial management, and ultimately, it is designed to inspire audacious advocates like you to bring their dreams to life. A successful law office isn't built overnight, but with the essential tips and information packed into this report, the task becomes less daunting and more exciting! Are you ready to shape your future in legal practice? Let this Special Report be your reliable companion on this journey.

Chapter 2. Understanding the Legal Landscape

Entering the world of legal practice requires more than just a thorough understanding of the laws and regulations. It demands an awareness of the broader landscape—both micro and macro—in which your future law office will operate. This includes an understanding of the current state of the industry, emerging trends, prospective clients' needs, and the overall environment affecting the legal sector.

2.1. The Current State of the Legal Industry

The last decade has seen a significant transformation in the legal industry. Driven by globalization, technological advancements, and changes in regulation and client expectations, legal service delivery has seen a major shift in recent times.

Today's legal industry consists of more than just traditional law firms. Alternative Legal Service Providers (ALSPs)—which include legal process outsourcers, contract and freelance attorneys, and legal tech startups—have gained a significant market share, offering competitive pricing and agile delivery methods.

Globalization has reshaped the way law firms operate. While local knowledge remains important, firms are increasingly required to adapt to international markets and legal systems. Regulatory changes, such as the liberalization of industries critical to your prospective clients, can create opportunities for innovative legal services.

2.2. Understanding Legal Service Innovation

Innovation has become a buzzword in today's legal industry. Technology has not only made legal services more efficient but has also transformed how they are delivered.

Lawtech startups have democratized access to legal services, making it easier for individuals and businesses to obtain legal assistance. Predictive analytics, machine learning, and AI are now used for tasks like legal research, document review, and even predicting court outcomes.

Understanding these changes is crucial for any new law firm. By leveraging technology, you can provide efficient, cost-effective services that meet your clients' evolving expectations.

2.3. Know Your Potential Client

Knowledge of the current state of the industry and service innovation should be accompanied by an understanding of potential clients.

Are you targeting individuals, small businesses, corporations, or non-profits? Know what kind of services your clients require and how they prefer them delivered. Do they value face-to-face communication? Are they comfortable using technology in the provision of legal services? Understanding your client's preferences and needs can inform your business model and determine your firm's success.

2.4. Analyzing Macroeconomic Factors

The wider economy significantly influences demand for legal services. Therefore, understanding prevailing economic conditions is imperative for any new law firm.

Widespread economic growth can boost demand for legal services, resulting in a proliferation of opportunities for law firms. However, a downturn can bring about an increase in the number of bankruptcy, restructuring, and litigation cases.

It is pivotal to consider these larger economic trends when strategically planning your law firm's establishment and growth.

2.5. Regulatory Environment

Every law firm is guided by a set of external regulations. Beyond just providing legal services, your firm will also have to abide by rules that govern business operations, information security, human resources, and marketing.

It's crucial to understand these regulatory aspects, which can significantly impact your firm's operations. Make sure to take a deep dive into the relevant laws and obligations in your jurisdiction.

2.6. SWOT Analysis

Performing a SWOT (Strengths, Weaknesses, Opportunities, and Threats) analysis can be a valuable tool in understanding the legal landscape. It can outline your firm's potential by analyzing your strengths and weaknesses, while considering opportunities and threats in your environment.

With a well-conducted SWOT analysis, you are better equipped to build a strategic plan that differentiates your firm in a competitive market, anticipates roadblocks, and capitalizes on openings.

2.7. Ethical Considerations

Lastly, but by no means least, a keen understanding of ethical considerations is crucial in the legal profession. Being true ambassadors of justice means adhering to the highest ethical standards - both towards your clients and in your interactions with the court, opposing counsel, and the public.

Understanding the legal landscape requires comprehensive knowledge of these and other areas. By remaining informed and adaptable, you can strategically position your firm to seize opportunities in the ever-changing world of legal practice. Remember, your success in the legal landscape depends as much on your knowledge and understanding of these factors as it is on your legal prowess.

Chapter 3. Establishing your Law Practice: The Basics

Understanding the legal landscape, and knowing what steps to take to set up your own law practice, are key to any successful legal start-up. To make the process easier, we've broken down the basics into key areas.

3.1. Building Your Business Model

Your business model is the foundation of your law practice. Having a clear vision for your practice, including your mission and values, will keep you focused on the right path. It is also important to identify your target clients, whether they are individuals or businesses. Understand your client's needs and expectations, and then plan your services to meet them. Your business model should also include clear financial projections and cash flow strategies.

3.2. Legal Structure and Compliance

When starting a law practice, the legal structure you choose for your business will have tax implications and will affect the amount of paperwork your business needs to do. The most straightforward type of business structure is a sole proprietorship. However, you can choose to form a partnership or a limited liability company, or even a corporation, depending on your preferred liability protection.

In addition, there are a number of legal compliances to fulfill. Depending on your region, this may include getting a business permit or license, getting insured, and perhaps even hiring a legal compliance officer for your practice.

3.3. Hiring Your Team

When you start your law practice, you might be able to manage all the work yourself. However, as your practice grows, you'll need to expand your team. Hiring the right people is critical in building a successful law practice. You need people who share your vision and can help your firm grow, whether they are attorneys, paralegals, legal assistants, or administrative staff.

3.4. Setting Up Your Office

Your office is the face of your law practice. Your office location, its accessibility, and its overall setup are often the first impressions clients get of your practice. Ideally, your office should be located in an accessible area where your target clients are located.

When setting up your office, consider what equipment you will need, such as a good phone system, enough computers, legal software, and office furniture. Your office environment should emphasize functionality and professionalism.

3.5. Marketing Your Law Practice

Marketing is crucial in establishing and growing your law practice. Building a strong online presence is particularly important in this digital age. Creating a website, optimizing it for search engines, and using social media to connect with potential clients are just some of the ways you can market your practice.

Also, consider traditional marketing methods, such as networking and referrals. Don't forget to focus on building relationships with your clients, as this can often lead to future referrals.

3.6. Finances and Accounting

A clear understanding of your firm's finances is critical in running a successful law practice. Start by creating a budget, and then monitor your income and expenses closely. You might want to hire an accountant or utilize good accounting software to help you stay on top of your finances.

Cash flow management is another critical aspect of running your law practice. Billing your clients accurately and on time, paying your expenses, and ensuring that you're paid on time are common challenges in managing cash flow.

3.7. Building Your Client Base

Last but not least, it's crucial to continuously focus on building your client base. This involves creating a strong network of contacts, actively seeking referrals, and delivering exceptional service to your existing clients to ensure they come back to you for future legal needs. Always keep your clients' best interests at heart, and work diligently to protect their rights and interests.

In conclusion, setting up your own law practice can be a rewarding experience. It offers independence and the potential for financial success, but it also requires diligence, discipline, and a clear understanding of the business side of running a law practice. Use the knowledge and strategies shared in this comprehensive guide to build a successful law practice that reflects your vision and meets your financial goals.

Chapter 4. Decoding Financial Management for Legal Firms

Managing finances is a critical aspect of running any business – and a law firm is no exception. Consistent monitoring of finance, cost-effectiveness, understanding the rates, and using the right billing techniques are significant for consistently maintaining the profitability of your legal firm. This chapter will provide you a deep insight into managing finances and securing profitability for your law firm.

4.1. Understanding the Fundamentals of Legal Firm Finances

Running a law firm is akin to managing a business entity. The fundamental rule for financial management is understanding the costs and the revenues.

The cost can primarily be segregated into fixed costs and variable costs. Fixed costs are those expenses that do not change and link not with the amount of legal service you provide to your clients. The primary components include rent for the office location, salaries of your employees, insurance, etc.

Variable costs, on the other hand, rely on the extent of your services. They include costs related to the specific legal services you provide and fluctuate depending on the number of cases you handle. Examples could be traveling for client meetings, witness fees, etc.

Being aware of cost structure is a fundamental aspect to ensure effective financial management and steering the financial direction of your law firm.

4.2. Methods and Systems for Legal Billing

Understanding effective billing methods can be the key turnstile for securing profitability and managing finances for your law firm.

1. Hourly rates: This is the most common form of billing wherein you charge your clients for each hour you dedicate towards their legal services. Standard hourly rates usually differ by the size of the firm, geographic location, and experience, among other factors.

2. Contingency fees: Widely used in personal injury, accident cases, or other litigation fields. In this method, the legal fee is a percentage of the amount the client is awarded.

3. Flat fees: In this system, you charge a fixed amount for providing specified legal services.

The choice of billing systems depends on several factors such as case type, client preference, the complexity of the legal issue, etc.

4.3. Strategic Pricing for Legal Services

Legal pricing involves complex considerations. Defining the right price entails contemplating factors like market dynamics, the prevalent rate for similar services in the industry, etc. Pricing your services too low can sabotage your profitability; however, too high a price may risk losing clients to your competitors—hence balance is crucial in this aspect.

Additionally, it's important to communicate the pricing methodology to your clients transparently. Misunderstandings regarding fees and charges are a significant reason for client dissatisfaction. It's fundamental to ensure your clients comprehend their payment responsibilities.

4.4. Cash Flow Management

Cash flow refers to the net amount of cash moving in and out of the law firm. Positive cash flow indicates that the firm's liquid assets are increasing—providing you with the means to cover expenses, reinvest in the business, and ensure business survival in the short-run. Therefore, effectively managing cash flow should be one of your top priorities.

1. Timely Billing: Ensure you are invoicing clients promptly. The quicker you bill, the quicker you can expect payment.

2. Follow-up payments: Implement a robust system to manage receivables.

3. Budget Forecasts: Create and regularly update budget forecasts.

4. Controlled Expenses: Always keep an eye on your expenses and ensure they are not spiraling out of control.

4.5. Embracing Technology: Legal Accounting Software

Legal accounting software can immensely aid in managing the finances of your law firm. A variety of software choices available today can help manage client budgets, trust accounts, billing, and general accounting.

Features might include:

1. Time-tracking

2. Trust accounting

3. Bill generation

4. General ledger accounting

5. Report generation

A well-chosen, specialized legal accounting software can help streamline your financial management efforts significantly.

4.6. Final Thoughts

Managing the finances of your law firm isn't merely an administrative task—it's a critical strategic function. Your profitability, cash flow management, and financial health rely upon it. An understanding of the costs and effectively managing the same, selecting a suitable billing method, defining competitive yet profitable pricing, managing cash flow, and leveraging legal accounting software for efficient and effective financial management are some of the key steps to decoding financial management for legal firms.

Remember, managing finances wisely is a step towards the successful operation of your law firm. With effective financial management principles and practices, your firm will be better prepared to overcome financial hurdles, increase profitability, and secure sustainable success.

Chapter 5. Ethics and Compliance in the Legal Business

The legal profession is built not only on the expertise and skills of its practitioners but also on its ethics and compliance with applicable laws and regulations. Running your own law office necessitates an intricate understanding and adherence to the ethical standards that govern the legal industry. This chapter delves into the significance of ethics and compliance in the legal business, how to establish an ethical culture in your law office, and practical strategies for staying compliant with laws, regulations, and professional standards.

5.1. Importance of Ethics in Legal business

Ethics forms the fundamental cornerstone of legal practice. They ensure integrity, trustworthiness, and professionalism, key traits sought by clients. In addition, adherence to ethical standards minimizes the risk of reputational damage, malpractice lawsuits, and disciplinary action by the regulatory bodies. The rules of professional conduct provide a roadmap to navigate ethical dilemmas that may arise. Therefore, it is imperative for every law office to be well-versed with these rules and incorporate them into everyday operations.

5.2. Understanding the Rules of Professional Conduct

Each jurisdiction may have its own specific regulatory body that enforces a set of rules for professional conduct. In the United States, for instance, this is often the state bar association. The Association of Professional Responsibility Lawyers (APRL), ABA's Model Rules of Professional Conduct, and local bar association guidelines provide a solid foundation for understanding your ethical obligations. Remember, knowledge of these rules isn't just nice-to-have; it's a fundamental prerequisite for running a law office.

5.3. Establishing an Ethical Culture

Creating an ethical culture within your law firm goes beyond just having a written code of conduct. Your actions and decisions, particularly those made in tough situations, act as a model to everybody else in the firm. It's important to:

- Regularly provide ethics training to your team members, so they know what to do when faced with an ethical conundrum.

- Have a clear and open line of communication to discuss professional ethics.

- Take swift and fair action if a violation of the ethical standards occurs.

An ethical work environment sets a tone of integrity and professionalism not just internally but also resonates with your clients and instills their trust in your law office.

5.4. Importance of Compliance in Legal Business

Compliance is a broad field and refers to abiding by the laws, rules, and professional standards applicable to your legal business. Non-compliance can lead to sanctions, fines, disbarment, and can severely damage your firm's reputation.

5.5. Areas of Compliance

There are numerous areas of compliance a law firm must be keenly aware of, including but not limited to:

- Legal Practice Regulations: You must comply with the legal practice rules of each jurisdiction where you provide services.

- Financial Regulations: Compliant bookkeeping and tax practices are critical to avoiding fiscal penalties and potential charges of fraud.

- Data Protection: Regulations around data protection and privacy have been tightened with laws such as the General Data Protection Regulation (GDPR) in the EU.

- Anti-Money Laundering (AML): AML compliance requires having internal policies, procedures, and controls to detect and report suspicious activities.

- Employment Laws: Being an employer means complying with many aspects of employment law, including safety regulations, workers' compensation, and equal employment opportunity laws.

5.6. Implementation and Monitoring Compliance

The first step in achieving compliance is to carry out a regulatory assessment that identifies the laws and rules that apply to your business model. From there, you can design relevant policies and procedures. The process doesn't end when these policies are implemented, however. Regular auditing and monitoring are necessary to ensure continual compliance.

5.7. Using Technology for Compliance

An array of software tools can simplify the compliance process. Various tools can help securely store and track client data, accurately track finances, and provide templates for standard legal documents. Due diligence software can streamline AML compliance. While technology can significantly ease the process, human oversight is always essential to ensure accuracy and thoroughness.

5.8. Conclusion

Ethics and compliance should be part of the foundation upon which your law office is built. Your adherence to the ethical standards and laws governing your practice provides a reassuring measure of your professionalism to your clients. It's an investment that ultimately earns dividends in the form of trust, reliability, and a reputation for professionalism. Ensure ethics and compliance are not just in your rule book, but in your actions and the underlying culture of your law office.

Chapter 6. Staffing and Management: Building a Strong Team

In the realm of law practice, your team becomes the heart of your firm. Staffing and management are crucial since you rely on your team, not only for their skill sets but also for their capacity to assist in maintaining and promoting your firm's brand and reputation.

6.1. Understanding Your Needs

First, it's crucial to understand your needs in terms of skills, expertise, and experience before you start hiring. Take a note of the current gaps in your firm's capability - this could include legal specializations, client management, or administrative tasks. Also, decide whether you wish to hire full-time employees or part-time consultants. Remember, your goal is to create a well-rounded team that can provide quality legal services and excellent client management.

Additionally, understand the roles that require immediate filling. An entry-level lawyer may be beneficial, but perhaps what you need more urgently is an office manager who can keep things running smoothly. Prioritize your staffing based on the immediate and long-term needs of your law practice.

6.2. Finding Potential Team Members

Next, you need to find potential team members. Networking events, law school alumni associations, online job portals, and recruitment agencies can be valuable sources. Take advantage of LinkedIn and other professional networking sites. Remember that your team members represent your firm, so look for candidates who not only meet your skill and experience requirements but also align with your firm's values and work culture.

6.3. Hiring the Right Candidates

Once you've identified potential candidates, the hiring process should be carefully managed. Interviews should not only assess a candidate's legal knowledge but also their problem-solving skills, communication abilities, work ethics, and their fit with your legal practice's culture.

If budget permits, invest in a professional hiring system or outsource hiring to reliable Human Resources firms with experience in legal staffing. They can help to streamline the process and ensure you are legally compliant.

6.4. Onboarding and Training

After hiring, a robust onboarding and training program can guide your new team members towards success. Start by introducing them to other staff members and familiarize them with the firm's culture, practices, and norms. Invest in their skills through professional development courses and encourage them to attend relevant law seminars.

Remember to train them in client management as well. The legal world is more than just cases and courtrooms - how your firm handles clients matter significantly.

6.5. Building a Cooperative Environment

Foster an inclusive work environment where everyone feels valued and heard. Regular meetings, open communication channels, and team building activities can build camaraderie and cooperation. Remember, the more productive the work environment, the more effectively your firm can serve clients.

It's also essential to establish a system for conflict resolution. Differences of opinion can arise in any workplace, and your legal practice isn't an exception. Having a clear dispute resolution protocol helps to keep your work environment harmonious and productive.

6.6. Performance Management and Growth Opportunities

Keep track of individual and team performance. Regular evaluations can identify strengths and areas that need improvement. Use this information to provide feedback, appreciate good work and offer coaching for improvement.

The possibility of career advancement is a powerful motivator. Provide a clear path for advancement in the firm for your employees and encourage them in their growth. Growth opportunities could include furthering their legal education, leading a team, or even becoming a partner in your firm in due time.

6.7. Compensation and Benefits

Lastly, ensure that your compensation and benefits are competitive. Besides the basic salary, benefits can include health insurance, paid time off, flexible work options, and retirement plans. Recognition for work well done, whether through incentives or awards, can boost morale and motivate your team towards excellence.

Comfortable working conditions, a healthy work-life balance, and options for remote work can also be effective in attracting and retaining quality staff.

Remember, your team is the backbone of your law firm. The time, effort, and resources invested into building a strong, competent, and satisfied team can pay dividends in terms of your successful law practice. It's an ongoing process, and there will always be room for improvement, but with a strong foundation in place, your firm will be well-positioned for success.

Chapter 7. Client Management: Establishing Loyalty and Trust

Establishing trust and loyalty with your clients is paramount in the legal profession, particularly when starting your own law firm. Building strong relationships doesn't only lead to patient interactions and smoother legal proceedings, but it also results in client retention and organic growth through word-of-mouth referrals. In an industry where reputation is crucial, this chapter lays out critical guidelines for nurturing relationships that lead to loyal clients that trust in your expertise.

7.1. Building Relationship with Clients

The foundation of any thriving law practice is the client-attorney relationship, which establishes trust and conditions for successful cooperation. As a service provider, your first goal should be to satisfy clients with their needs and expectations. This starts with understanding the stakes of each case, the client's goals, and with it, their fears and challenges. Address these concerns upfront, always prioritizing transparent communication to nurture trust and loyalty.

7.2. Effective Communication

Communication is at the heart of any relationship, especially between a client and their attorney. The goal of effective communication is clear and concise information delivery, allowing clients to understand the procedures, potentials, threats, and strategies associated with their case. Legal jargon can often be confusing to those not practicing law; therefore, explain complex legal procedures in a language that clients can easily comprehend. Regularly update them about case progression to avoid any communication gap that could potentially hamper trust.

7.3. Client Engagement and Interaction

Clients appreciate attention and responsiveness in their legal representation. Engaging with clients involves not only frequent updates but also active listening and empathizing. Understanding and acknowledging their concerns can prove decisive in developing lasting relationships. Strive to be approachable, accessible, and responsive in this digital era where client interaction has largely gone online; prompt email responses, phone calls, or scheduled virtual meetings can make a significant impact.

7.4. Maintaining Confidentiality and Professionalism

Maintaining a professional demeanor is critical in any business, and it's even more vital in legal practice. Always treat clients with respect irrespective of the size or type of their case. Confidentiality is a cornerstone of the attorney-client relationship. Create a safe environment for clients to share sensitive information by implementing robust security measures for physical and digital data. This safeguards not only clients' trust but also your firm's reputation.

7.5. Conflict Management and Resolution

Constructive conflict resolution can significantly impact client loyalty and trust. Be transparent about potential conflicts of interest from the outset to maintain honesty in the relationship. Use your skills to mediate during conflicts that may arise during proceedings as this gives reassurance to clients of your control and expertise.

7.6. Delivering on Promises

Nothing breaks trust faster than making promises you cannot keep. Be honest about what you can deliver and what the realistic outcome of a situation may be. When expectations are set realistically, clients are less likely to be dissatisfied, leading to stronger, more forgivable relationships.

7.7. Feedback Mechanism

Implementing a feedback mechanism allows not only a chance for continuous improvement but also offers clients an opportunity to voice their concerns. This simple practice can dramatically impact how your clients perceive their importance in your firm and can act as a catalyst to improve trust levels.

Conclusion

Creating and nurturing a loyal client base that trusts your firm is a journey with no destination. It's a constant cycle of learning, adapting, and implementing the best solutions for your clients, and it's paramount to your practice's success. As you develop these habits and incorporate them into your practice, you will notice an improvement in client satisfaction, loyalty, and overall growth of your practice.

Chapter 8. Marketing and Networking for Law Practices

Understanding the inextricable link between marketing and networking can greatly influence the success of your law practice. Realizing the value derived from proficiently marketing your services and resources, as well as building an expansive network, is critical in staying competitive in today's legal ecosystem.

8.1. Marketing Strategies for a Successful Law Practice

Successful marketing in legal practice is a combination of creativity, effective communication, and strategic planning. It is not about the amount spent, rather, it is about targeting the right audience with a tailored message.

First, identify your unique selling proposition (USP). This is what makes your practice different and more appealing than others. A compelling USP creates a strong market presence and will guide your marketing strategies.

Develop your brand. This should be a clear representation of you, your practice, and your values. Consistency in your brand, including your logo, colors, and tone of voice, will make your law practice more recognizable and memorable.

An online presence is crucial in today's digital world. Create an easy-to-navigate website featuring information about you, your specialty areas, testimonials, and relevant content for visitors. Complement this with active profiles on suitable social media platforms.

Content marketing is a powerful tool for legal practitioners. Sharing relevant and informative legal articles or blog posts positions you as an expert in your field, facilitates client education, and drives website traffic.

Pay-per-click advertising, while potentially more costly, can be a highly effective form of marketing for law practices. These ads, targeted at search keywords related to your practice area and region, can generate immediate visibility among prospective clients.

Finally, monitoring and evaluating your marketing strategies is crucial in identifying what works and what doesn't. Use analysis tools to guide future marketing efforts.

8.2. The Power of Networking

Networking, both online and offline, should be an integral part of your marketing strategy. Building relationships in the industry garners support, while client networks generate referrals.

Engage with professional community events, legal committees, or local business meetings. Also consider joining professional organizations relevant to your practice area.

Having a strong online network, particularly on professional networking sites, can help build your reputation and visibility. Join industry relevant online forums and social media groups to share your knowledge, learn, and network simultaneously.

The power of networking also relies on maintaining relationships. Regular follow-ups ensure that you stay top of mind for referrals or future collaborations.

8.3. The Role of Client Satisfaction in Marketing

Client satisfaction can be a significant marketing tool. Positive experiences encourage clients to share their interactions with their personal networks. Seek testimonials and reviews from satisfied clients to use in your marketing efforts.

Always ask for referrals. Satisfied clients are often willing to recommend you, particularly if asked directly. Offering a referral program as an incentive can also boost your chances of gaining new clients.

8.4. Utilizing Technology in Marketing and Networking

In our technology-driven world, utilizing the right tools can make your marketing and networking efforts more productive and cost-effective.

Customer relationship management (CRM) systems can track your interactions with current and potential clients, helping you maintain relationships and garner future business.

Marketing automation tools can streamline your marketing processes and make them more targeted and efficient. Similarly, social media management tools can save time with post scheduling and analytical capabilities.

Legal directories are a great place to list your practice online, as many potential clients use these for their searches.

8.5. Summing Up

Marketing is not a one-time effort, it is essential to continuously promote your law practice while cultivating and nurturing your professional network. Teaming a strong marketing strategy with an expansive network can greatly promote your law practice and set you up for success.

A formula for success includes executing a well-thought marketing plan, having a strong online presence, participating in networking events, investing time in nurturing relationships, utilizing technology, and prioritizing client satisfaction.

Sounds daunting? Remember, you do not have to do it all at once. Start small and build from there, and every step taken is a step toward your law practice's success.

Chapter 9. Addressing Risks and Challenges in Legal Business

Running a law firm comes with inherent risks and challenges. As with any other business, there is always the potential for unforeseeable and often controllable factors that can either make or break your endeavor. However, the key lies in proper planning, preparing for the worst, and having proactive strategies.

9.1. Risk Identification

Recognizing potential risks is the first critical step in risk management and mitigation. Identifying risks involves monitoring potential threats that could harm your firm financially or reputationally. These could range from changes in laws, client dissatisfaction, poor financial management, to technological challenges.

9.2. Financial Risks

Financial threats and complications can arise from several different areas. Your law firm could experience low or fluctuating cash flow, significant expenses, lack of profitability, or could even face potential bankruptcy.

Managing cash flow: A main risk associated with legal practices is maintaining a healthy cash flow. Fees from clients may not come in quickly, but operating expenses must continually be paid. Implementing policies to speed up payment collection, such as requiring deposits or moving to a flat fee billing structure, can help mitigate this risk.

Financial management: Poor financial management can lead to substantial risks, including a lack of profitability. Recognizing the need for sound financial practices and investing in a good financial manager or accountant can help keep your firm's finances on track.

Planning for unexpected expenses: Ensuring that you have funds set aside for unforeseen costs is an important aspect of risk management. This reserve could be used to cover any unexpected costs that are not covered by your firm's regular cash flow, such as litigation costs.

9.3. Operational Risks

Operational risks pertain to your law firm's day-to-day operations and may arise due to inefficient systems, inadequate resources, poor management, or changes in laws and regulations.

Operational efficiency: Inefficient operations can put your firm at risk of losing clients, personnel, and financial stability. Processes such as client onboarding, work allocation, and billing should be streamlined to prevent operational hiccups.

Changes in law: Legal practices are highly sensitive to changes in laws and regulations. Keeping a strict watch on imminent changes and preparing to adapt is imperative. Employing a dedicated compliance officer or team can be a beneficial strategy.

9.4. Technological Risks

In the digital age, technology is an integral part of running a successful law firm. From managing client records to executing digital marketing strategies, technology can be a boon or a bane. Technological risks could involve inadequate use of technology, lack of digital security, or loss of data.

Embrace technology: Failing to adapt to new technologies can put your law firm at a severe disadvantage. Utilize dedicated software for legal practice management to enhance efficiency and productivity. Keeping an eye on technological advances can also help you stay ahead of the competition.

Cybersecurity: In the age of cyber threats, ensuring your firm's and clients' confidential data are protected is of utmost importance. Invest in reliable cybersecurity measures and ensure all staff members are aware of best practices.

9.5. Reputation Risks

The reputation of your law firm plays a significant role in its success. Poor reviews from clients, disciplinary action from a legal services regulator, damaged relationships with personnel, and negative media publicity can potentially harm your firm's reputation.

Client satisfaction: Building a robust relationship with your clients and ensuring their satisfaction is critical. Unhappy clients are more likely to leave negative reviews and deter potential clients.

Management of personnel: In addition to managing client relationships effectively, maintaining your relationships with your employees, associates, and partners is just as important. Treating your staff well leads to a motivated and productive team, while poor management can lead to high turnover rates, reduced productivity, and negative reviews.

9.6. Risk Mitigation Strategies

Identifying risks is not enough, they need to be managed and mitigated with carefully planned strategies. These include:

Proper Planning: Investigate and deeply understand potential risks before they turn into crises. Develop detailed strategies that precisely outline how each risk will be managed.

Insurance: Many risks can be assuaged by having suitable insurance coverage. Obtain professional indemnity insurance to protect against potential negligence claims.

Training: Continual skill and knowledge training for yourself and your staff can be an efficient way of managing operational and business risks. This could include training in practice management, financial management, client service, ethics, and technology.

Running a law practice is a complex process, filled with both exciting and challenging moments. However, understanding the risks, identifying potential obstacles, and implementing necessary mitigations can go a long way in creating a profitable and sustainable legal practice. Stay vigilant, adapt, and be prepared to brave all storms that might arise in your legal endeavor. The resilience you build in the process is your pathway to success.

Chapter 10. Boosting Profitability: Proven Strategies and Techniques

Boosting Profitability: Proven Strategies and Techniques

To increase the profitability of your law office, a multitude of techniques should be considered and employed, several of which will be explored in depth in the following text.

10.1. Efficient Billing Practices

Efficient billing practices are a prerequisite to profitable law practice. Attention to detail and maintaining accurate data is extremely important to law firms because they bill by the hour. Certain strategies can be employed to optimize use of billable hours.

Time Tracking: The use of reliable time tracking software allows for easier, faster, and more accurate record of the number of billable hours accumulated by lawyers each day.

Transparency: A well-maintained billing system supports transparency in your law office. Clients must clearly understand what they are paying for; providing itemized billing statements enables clients to see the direct correlation between your services and the fees charged.

10.2. Adopt and Leverage Technology

With technological advancements revolutionising all business sectors, the legal services sector is no exception. To increase profitability, law firms should embrace the adoption of modern, efficient technology.

Case Management Software: Case management software streamlines and coordinates various aspects of a case, saving time and ensuring that all information is easily available when necessary.

Artificial Intelligence (AI): AI tools can help automate repetitive tasks such as drafting contracts and legal research that would otherwise consume a significant amount of billable hours.

Cloud Storage: Secure cloud storage services can provide a cost-effective solution for information storage and file sharing. It can also ensure secure access to data remotely.

10.3. Strategic Marketing

Effective marketing strategies can be instrumental in bolstering the profitability of your law office.

Digital Marketing: Social media, email newsletters and search engine optimization are not only modern marketing practices, but also more cost-effective than traditional marketing means.

Website: A user-friendly website showcasing areas of expertise, detailed lawyer profiles, case studies and customer testimonials can help prospective clients get a better understanding and increase trust in your services.

10.4. Diversify Service Offerings

Expanding your areas of practice may enable you to garner more clients and increase profitability. Be careful to train and educate your staff in the new practice areas to maintain service quality.

Leveraging Expertise: Capitalize on the existing areas of expertise by offering consultation and advisory services, workshops or webinars.

Collaborations: Collaborations or partnerships with other legal or non-legal businesses can help you in winning larger contracts or gaining access to new customer markets.

10.5. Client Relationship Management

A loyal and satisfied customer is the best business strategy of all. A dedicated client will bring repeat business and referrals for your company.

Client Satisfaction: Prioritize the satisfaction of your clients. Clients' opinions should be highly valued, and feedback should be used to improve services.

Communication: Regular, open communication with clients can build trust and confidence. Establishing a responsive, reliable line of communication can set client's minds at ease.

10.6. Continual Professional Development

Continual professional development (CPD) of you and your staff is an investment that can significantly increase the productivity and profitability of your law office.

Training and Workshops: Regular training sessions and workshops should be organized to keep staff updated with the latest laws, technologies, and practices.

Learning Culture: Cultivating a culture of continuous learning will encourage staff members to develop their skills and qualifications, potentially enhancing your services and efficiency over time.

Remember, boosting the profitability in the legal services sector is a challenging but potentially rewarding endeavor. By incorporating these proven strategies and techniques, you'll lay a strong foundation for a financially thriving law office.

Chapter 11. Looking Ahead: Ensuring Sustainability and Growth

Your law firm is a business and, like any other business, needs a strategic course to ensure sustainability and growth. The way you project your business forward will have a considerable impact on your law firm's success. Let's delve into the details of planning and establishing a concrete direction for your firm.

11.1. Creating a Strategic Business Plan

A strategic business plan outlines your law firm's future course of action and creates a foundation upon which your venture can grow and prosper. Your firm's business plan should incorporate your vision, milestones for growth, financial objectives, and marketing strategies. Incorporating these into your business plan will help provide a sense of direction and purpose for your law firm.

Financial projections and budgets form a crucial part of your law firm's strategic business plan, guiding your revenue generation and expense management. Sound financial management ensures your firm's sustainability in the long-term.

Remember, the business plan is not set in stone. The legal market and your firm will change over time. It should be flexible enough to enable necessary adjustments and modifications.

11.2. Client Relationship Management

Your clients are the lifeblood of your firm. Ensuring their satisfaction and loyalty is therefore crucial to your practice's growth. Effective client relationship management involves regular communication, delivering excellent service, and asking for referrals.

Keeping clients informed about their case developments, changes in laws applicable to them, and other relevant information not only fosters trust but also enhances your firm's reputation. Likewise, asking satisfied clients to refer your services to others can lead to new business avenues.

11.3. Enhancing Your Expertise

With the ever-evolving nature of law and sporadic changes in regulations, proactively enhancing your expertise is crucial. Regular learning and staying at the forefront of your practice area ensures you provide the best possible advice and service to your clients.

11.4. Leveraging Technology

In today's digital era, leveraging technology is not optional; it is necessary. Technology can help your firm streamline operations, increase efficiency, improve client service, enhance data security, and eventually contribute to your firm's growth. From legal research to client management, record-keeping to billing, technology enhances all aspects of your practice.

11.5. Marketing Your Law Firm

A well-formulated and executed marketing strategy plays a critical role in your law firm's growth. From networking and referral building to online marketing and harnessing social media, there are various ways your law firm can gain prominence and draw in new clients.

11.6. Building a Solid Team

Surrounding yourself with a competent team not only eases your workload but also helps boost your firm's productivity and profitability. Your team should share your vision and work towards your law firm's collective success.

11.7. Evaluating and Improving

Conduct regular audits of your firm's performance to assess what's working and what isn't. These audits can encompass financial performance, client satisfaction, marketing efficacy, staff performance, and more. Based on these evaluations, changes and improvements can be applied to continue the growth trajectory.

11.8. Planning for Succession

Succession planning, while often overlooked, should be an integral part of your law firm's growth strategy. Identify potential leaders, transfer knowledge, and cultivate necessary skills to ensure your law firm continues to thrive even after your departure.

In conclusion, ensuring your law firm's sustainability and growth requires thorough planning and execution. Leveraging the above strategies, you can equip your firm to navigate the legal marketplace's challenges and set the stage for enduring success.

www.ingramcontent.com/pod-product-compliance
Lightning Source LLC
Chambersburg PA
CBHW072218290526
45794CB00007B/2792